DISCOVER
FOOTBA
GROUNDS
FROM ABOVE

Above: the City Ground, home of Nottingham Forest, sited between the Notts County ground and the
Trent Bridge county cricket ground.

PHOTOGRAPHS BY

TEXT BY CASSANDRA WELLS

MYRIAD
LONDON

ARSENAL

Arsenal started life as a team called Dial Square in 1886, based in Woolwich, south-east London. They changed their name to Royal Arsenal in 1887 and to Woolwich Arsenal in 1891. Their early games were played on Woolwich Common but they moved to Manor Field in 1888, where they remained for the next 26 years. Despite being successful in the League, which they joined in 1893, their gates were low and they went into voluntary liquidation in 1910. Henry Norris, owner of Fulham FC, bought the struggling club and moved them to Highbury, north London, in 1913 much to the annoyance of their neighbours Spurs and Clapton Orient. After WWI Arsenal rejoined the First Division, where they have remained since 1919. Architect Claude Waterlow Ferrier was commissioned to design a stadium for Arsenal, and he set about using an Art Deco style for the ground. In 1931 he extended the terraces at each end, and began building the West Stand. The 1930s also saw success on the pitch; Arsenal won the League five times and the FA Cup twice. In

1935 an AFC monogrammed roof was added to the Laundry End Terrace; in the same season a record attendance of 73,295 turned out to see Arsenal take on Sunderland. In 1936 the East Stand was replaced and looked almost identical to Ferrier's West Stand. The 1970s saw more seats installed at Highbury, and further development came in the 1980s when the club added executive boxes to the Clock End. In 1991 the club drew up plans to rebuild the North Stand in order to increase capacity. The club had to play in front of just three stands in the 1992/93 season as the bulldozers moved in and a mural took the place of the fans on the North Bank. The new two-tiered North Stand opened in 1993. The Clock End and the East and West Terraces were next to be developed bringing a total capacity of 38,500 all-seated. At the beginning of the 2006/7 season Arsenal moved into the new Emirates Stadium. The new ground, just five minutes from Highbury at Ashburton Grove, consists of a four-tiered bowl with an all-seater capacity of 60,432.

GROUND: **Emirates Stadium**
ADDRESS: Highbury House, 75 Drayton Park, London N5 1BU
MAIN TEL: 020 7704 4000
BOX OFFICE: 020 7704 4040
WEBSITE: www.arsenal.com
HOME COLOURS: red shirts with white sleeves, white shorts with red trim, white and red hooped socks
CLUB NICKNAME: the Gunners
CAPACITY: 60,432
RECORD ATTENDANCE: (at the Emirates Stadium) 60,132 vs Reading, March 3 2007
PITCH DIMENSIONS: 105m x 68m (115 x 74 yards)
MOST PROLIFIC SCORER: Thierry Henry (226)
RECORD WIN: 12-0 vs Loughborough Town, March 12 1900
RECORD DEFEAT: 0-8 vs Loughborough Town, December 8 1896

ASTON VILLA

Aston Villa was formed by members of the Villa Cross Wesleyan Chapel in 1874. The club moved to the Aston Lower grounds in 1896 after spending 20 years at a basic ground on Wellington Road. The site was a leisure park dating back to the 1870s but had fallen into a state of disrepair. Villa began developing the ground, building a main stand on what had been a sub-tropical garden. Banking was raised on the other three sides of the ground and a basic barrel roof was added to the Trinity Road side. The ground opened in 1897, the same year Villa won the League and Cup double. Attendances continued to rise and prior to WWI the club was drawing in regular crowds of 26,000. In 1914 Villa realised their plans for future development of the ground. The work began with the removal of the concrete cycle path, which had run around the pitch; both end terraces were banked and another terrace added to the front of the Witton Lane Stand. After the war the

Trinity Road Stand was built, a stand which was so extravagant in design that it cost the club £89,810. The Holte End was extended during WWII, and in 1946 Villa Park saw its highest ever crowd of 76,588. Villa Park's selection as a location for World Cup games brought about further development with seats being added to the ground's terracing. The two-tiered North Stand was built in 1977, with further development coming in the light of the Taylor report. In 1990 the Holte End terracing was updated and the roof extended but as a result of poor planning the whole structure had to be demolished in 1994 and replaced with a two-tier stand. Trinity Road Stand was refurbished in time for the 1996 European Championships. In order to maintain a capacity in excess of 40,000 the club set about planning to redevelop the Witton Lane Stand (now the Doug Ellis Stand). There are plans to redevelop and enlarge the North Stand.

GROUND: **Villa Park**
ADDRESS: **Villa Park, Birmingham B6 6HE**
MAIN TEL: **0121 327 2299**
BOX OFFICE: **0121 327 5353**
WEBSITE: **www.avfc.co.uk**
CAPACITY: **42,551**
HOME COLOURS: **claret shirts with blue trim, white shorts with claret and blue trim, blue socks with white turnover**
CLUB NICKNAMES: **the Villans, Villa**
PITCH DIMENSIONS: **105m x 69m (115 x 72 yards)**
FOUNDED: **1874**
RECORD ATTENDANCE: **76,588 vs Derby County, March 2 1946**
MOST PROLIFIC SCORER: **Harry Hampton (215)**
RECORD WIN: **13-0 vs Wednesbury Old Athletic, October 30 1886**
RECORD DEFEAT: **0-7 vs Blackburn Rovers, October 19 1899**

BIRMINGHAM CITY

Birmingham City started as the Small Heath Alliance in 1875. Their first pitch was on waste ground on Arthur Street but as their crowd of followers grew, they moved to Muntz Street, where they remained for the next 29 years. The club turned professional in 1885 and changed their name to Birmingham FC in 1905. The Blues moved to St Andrews in 1906, onto a ground that had been previously occupied by gypsies, who are said to have laid a curse on it. The massive main stand was built and in order to raise the height of the ground beneath terracing on the Coventry Road End, locals were encouraged to dump rubbish on the site. A Kop terrace was built on top, with a capacity of 48,000. Terrace covers were put on top of the Railway End and the Kop by the time the ground recorded its highest gate ever of 66,844 in 1939. During WWII the curse returned, the ground was damaged by bombs over 20 times and the Main Stand burned down when a fireman inadvertently used petrol instead of water to put out a brazier. Birmingham had to move, first to Leamington and then Villa Park until 1943, while their ground was repaired. They emerged from the war with a new name, Birmingham City FC. The Kop reopened in 1947 and the new two-tiered Main Stand opened in 1954. Success in Europe funded the building of the Railway End Stand in 1963-4. The 1980s saw a run of bad luck, and by 1989 the Blues found themselves in the Third Division. March 1993 saw the Blues' fortunes improve as David Sullivan took over ownership of the club. Sullivan drew up plans for a £4.5million development of the Kop and Tilton Road End, which opened in 1994. In 1999 the Railway End was redeveloped and there are plans to develop the Main Stand sometime in the future.

GROUND: **St Andrews**
ADDRESS: **St Andrews Ground, Birmingham B9 4NH**
MAIN TEL: **0844 557 1875**
BOX OFFICE: **0844 557 1875**
WEBSITE: **www.bcfc.com**
CAPACITY: **30,016**
HOME COLOURS: **blue shirts, blue shorts, blue and white socks**
CLUB NICKNAME: **the Blues**
PITCH DIMENSIONS: **105m x 69m (115 x 75 yards)**
FOUNDED: **1875**
RECORD ATTENDANCE: **66,844 vs Everton, February 11 1939**
MOST PROLIFIC SCORER: **Joe Bradford (249)**
RECORD WIN: **12-0 vs Walsall T. Swifts, December 17 1892**
RECORD DEFEAT: **1-9 vs Sheffield Wednesday, December 13 1930**

BLACKBURN ROVERS

Blackburn Rovers were formed in 1875 by a group of former public schoolboys. It took the club a year before they settled at their first ground, Oozehead, to play regular matches. The club moved a further four times before settling at Ewood Park in 1890. During this time they had become the first real giants of English football, winning the FA Cup three years in a row from 1884 and again in 1890. In 1905 Laurence Cotton, a textile baron, set about transforming the ground. Between 1905-1914 he spent an estimated £12,000 on players and £33,000 on ground improvements. First came a pitched roof on the Darwen End, followed by the building of the Main Stand and the Nuttall Street Stand. Further improvements in 1914 came after Rovers had won the League title, when the Riverside Stand was built. By 1913 the capacity was 70,866. Little changed at the ground until 1960, when a Cup final appearance helped to fund a cantilevered roof over the Blackburn End. In 1980 safety regulations brought the capacity at Ewood Park down to 23,400 and tough times followed. In 1983 just 3,797 turned up to see the last game of the season. Fire checks in 1985 saw the upper tier of the Riverside End and the terrace below closed. In 1987 Rovers' fortunes improved and chairman Bill Fox persuaded his friend Jack Walker to help rebuild the Riverside Stand. This would be the start of a remarkable relationship. In 1991 Walker decided to buy a 62 per cent share in the Rovers and spent £13m on the team in his first 18 months. He then drew up plans for the building of three two-tiered stands. The building work incensed some locals, as houses and a local mill would need to be demolished. Regardless of this, the council approved the plans and in 1993 the developments began. When the Jack Walker Stand was opened in November 1994, the capacity was up to 31,367.

GROUND: **Ewood Park**
ADDRESS: **Ewood Park, Blackburn, Lancashire BB2 4JF**
MAIN TEL: **0871 702 1875**
BOX OFFICE: **0871 222 1444**
WEBSITE: **www.rovers.co.uk**
CAPACITY: **31,367**
HOME COLOURS: **blue and white halved shirts, white shorts with a blue trim, white socks with blue trim**
CLUB NICKNAME: **Rovers**
PITCH DIMENSIONS: **105m x 69m (115 x 76 yards)**
FOUNDED: **1875**
RECORD ATTENDANCE: **62,522 vs Bolton Wanderers, March 2 1929**
MOST PROLIFIC SCORER: **Simon Gurner (168)**
RECORD WIN: **11-0 vs Rossendale, October 13 1884**
RECORD DEFEAT: **0-8 vs Arsenal, February 25 1933**

BOLTON WANDERERS

Bolton Wanderers started as a Sunday school team called Christ Church FC, playing on Park Recreation Ground. They moved to Dick Cockle's Field on Pikes Lane in 1877, where the club had a row with the vicar and left to become Bolton Wanderers. In 1881 they moved to a proper sports ground on Pikes Lane, which had two small stands. In 1893 rising rents led Wanderers to bid farewell to Pikes Lane and build a new ground on wasteland. That ground, Burnden Park, would remain home to the Trotters for 102 years. Wanderers were one of the 12 founding members of the Football League, although the League title is one they have never won. Their success has always been with the FA Cup, a prize they have won four times, the last time being in 1958 when

GROUND: **Reebok Stadium**
ADDRESS: Reeebok Stadium, Burnden Way, Lostock, Bolton BL6 6JW
MAIN TEL: 01204 673 673
BOX OFFICE: 0871 871 2932
WEBSITE: www.bwfc.co.uk
CAPACITY: 28,723
HOME COLOURS: white shirts, navy shorts, navy socks
CLUB NICKNAME: the Trotters
PITCH DIMENSIONS: 105m x 68m (115 x 74 yards)
FOUNDED: 1874
RECORD ATTENDANCE: (at Burnden Park) 69,912 vs Manchester City, February 18 1933
MOST PROLIFIC SCORER: Nat Lofthouse (255)
RECORD WIN: 13-0 vs Sheffield United, February 1 1890
RECORD DEFEAT: 1-9 vs Preston North End, December 12 1887

Trotters legend Nat Lofthouse scored both of Bolton's goals against Manchester United. Their first attempt at winning the FA Cup came in 1904 however, and despite losing the final, the money raised meant they could build a main stand and terrace and cover the Great Lever End. The 1920s saw three FA Cup wins for Bolton, and again more ground improvements followed with the new Burnden Stand being built. Little changed at the ground for the following 70 years. The 1980s were the next major period of change for the club, as their fortunes had faded, and the club had sunk from the First Division to the Fourth. Crowds dropped to an all time low of 2,902 and, to raise revenue, the Trotters sold some of their land at the Railway End to a local superstore. By the 1990s, Bolton's fortunes had reversed; they reached the Premiership in 1995 and made plans for a 28,700 all-seater stadium. The impressive Reebok Stadium opened in 1997, the same season Colin Todd took the club back to the Premiership.

BURNLEY

Burnley was formed from a rugby team in 1882 and was known as Burnley Rovers for its first year of existence. In 1883, after dropping "Rovers" from their name, they moved to Turf Moor, where the club remains. The first stand to be built was an 800-seater stand on the south side and covers were added to each end. In 1908 the club built the Main Stand along one side and the so-called Star Stand on the other side. The team was well-supported and in 1924 recorded its highest ever attendance with 54,775 fans packing in to see the Clarets take on Huddersfield in the FA Cup. Between the wars concrete terracing was added to the Long Side Terrace and a roof was added in 1954. The club continued to develop the stands and seats, together with underfloor heating, were added to the Cricket Field End in 1969. The system of heating was extremely expensive and was done away with just two years later. A new single-tiered main stand was opened in 1974, named the Bob Lord Stand after the club's chairman. The Taylor report saw more changes at Turf Moor: the much-loved Long Side Terrace was cleared and the North Stand built in its place, a two-tiered cantilevered structure with 8,000 seats. A second two-tiered stand was also built at the east end of the ground, bringing capacity up to 22,546. There are plans for the club to develop the Cricket Field Stand by buying land currently owned by the cricket club.

GROUND: **Turf Moor**
ADDRESS: **Turf Moor, Harry Potts Way, Burnley BB10 4BX**
MAIN TEL: **0870 443 1882**
BOX OFFICE: **0870 443 1914**
WEBSITE: **www.burnleyfootballclub.com**
CAPACITY: **22,546**
HOME COLOURS: **claret and Sky shirt, white shorts, white socks**
CLUB NICKNAME: **the Clarets**
PITCH DIMENSIONS: **105m x 67m (115 x 73 yards)**
FOUNDED: **1882**
RECORD ATTENDANCE: **54,775 vs Huddersfield, February 23 1924**
MOST PROLIFIC SCORER: **George Beel (178)**
RECORD WIN: **9-0 vs Darwen, January 9 1892**

CELTIC

Celtic was formed in 1888 as a charitable trust for the Catholic communities in Glasgow's East End. The club played games at a ground called Celtic Park from 1888 until 1892. When they could no longer afford the rent, they moved to a former brickyard in Parkhead and took the name Celtic Park to their new home. The club quickly built a grandstand and a pavilion with terracing on both ends. In 1898 the club's director James Grant paid for the Grant Stand to be built; this was unusual in that it was on stilts and had padded seats and windows along the front and side. The Grant Stand was demolished in 1929 and the South Stand built in its place. By 1938 Celtic Park recorded its largest ever crowd of 92,000 in an Old Firm clash with Rangers. The next major changes to the ground took place between 1957-71, reflecting the success the Bhoys were having on the pitch. The Rangers End was covered following Celtic's European Cup triumph in 1967. In 1986 the club added a new front to the South Stand in readiness for the club's centenary; however Celtic's reluctance to add more seats cost them dear in the aftermath of the Hillsborough disaster. Celtic's debts were high and a plan was announced to move the club to a new 52,000 all-seater stadium. The fans were not keen and began boycotting games. As debts soared, the club faced receivership until Fergus McCann, a Canadian businessman, took over the club. He ditched the planned move and began developing Celtic Park into an all-seater stadium. Now the ground is fully enclosed, with three new two-tier stands and the older Main Stand bringing the capacity up to 60,832.

GROUND: **Celtic Park**
ADDRESS: **Celtic Park, Glasgow G40 3RE**
MAIN TEL: **0871 226 1888**
BOX OFFICE: **0871 226 1888**
WEBSITE: **www.celticfc.net**
CAPACITY: **60,832**
HOME COLOURS: **emerald green and white hooped shirts, white shorts with green trim, white socks**
CLUB NICKNAME: **the Bhoys**
PITCH DIMENSIONS: **105m x 68m (115 x 74 yards)**
FOUNDED: **1888**
RECORD ATTENDANCE: **92,000 vs Rangers, January 1 1938**
MOST PROLIFIC SCORER: **James McGrory (397)**
RECORD WIN: **11-0 vs Dundee, October 10 1895**
RECORD DEFEAT: **0-8 vs Motherwell, April 30 1937**

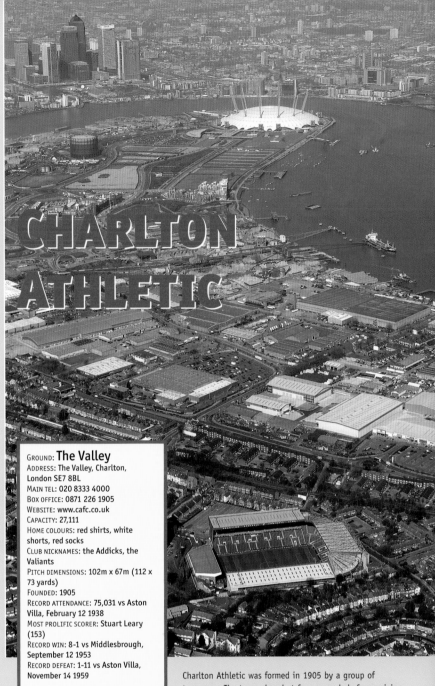

CHARLTON ATHLETIC

GROUND: **The Valley**
ADDRESS: The Valley, Charlton, London SE7 8BL
MAIN TEL: 020 8333 4000
BOX OFFICE: 0871 226 1905
WEBSITE: www.cafc.co.uk
CAPACITY: 27,111
HOME COLOURS: red shirts, white shorts, red socks
CLUB NICKNAMES: the Addicks, the Valiants
PITCH DIMENSIONS: 102m x 67m (112 x 73 yards)
FOUNDED: 1905
RECORD ATTENDANCE: 75,031 vs Aston Villa, February 12 1938
MOST PROLIFIC SCORER: Stuart Leary (153)
RECORD WIN: 8-1 vs Middlesbrough, September 12 1953
RECORD DEFEAT: 1-11 vs Aston Villa, November 14 1959

Charlton Athletic was formed in 1905 by a group of teenagers. The team played at four grounds before arriving at The Valley in 1919. At the time The Valley was a chalk and sand pit known as "the swamp". Volunteers helped to dig out a pitch and banking was formed at either end. By 1921, when the club had turned professional and built the Main Stand on the west side of the pitch, the ground was famed for its vast East Terrace. In 1923 the club decided to leave The Valley and move to a ground called The Mount. Charlton moved back to The Valley after just one season. The club had run up huge debts and were facing a bleak future until the Gliksten brothers stepped in with a £100,000 rescue package in 1931. Success on the pitch under the management of Jimmy Seed saw the fan base swell and in 1938 The Valley recorded its highest ever gate of 75,031. Despite winning the FA Cup in 1947, the club did not carry out any further development until 1950 when a few hundred seats were added to the Main Stand paddock. In the 1980s the club announced plans to make the ground all-seater. However, poor financial decisions meant Charlton had to leave The Valley in 1985 and moved in with local rivals Crystal Palace. New directors and a massive campaign by the club's dedicated fans led to an announcement in 1989 that Charlton would be moving back to The Valley. Fans and directors alike helped clear the overgrown pitch but in 1990 Greenwich Council turned down the plans. After forming a political party, the fans finally achieved their goal and despite having to spend a further season at Upton Park, the club moved back to The Valley in 1992. Since then the ground has been totally redeveloped with the large single-tiered East Stand and two-tiered North and West Stands: the Jimmy Seed Stand remains a small single-tiered structure. The north-east and north-west corners have been filled in and there are plans for the redevelopment of the Jimmy Seed Stand to eventually bring capacity to 40,000.

CHELSEA

Chelsea was formed in 1905, but the club's ground, Stamford Bridge, came into being almost 30 years earlier in 1877, when the London Athletic Club developed it as a running track from an orchard and market garden. In 1904 Gus Mears took over the ownership of the ground and developed it into a venue for cycling, athletics and football. Mears contracted Scottish architect, Archibald Leitch, to design the 5,000-seater Main Stand. Mears and his friend Fred Parker established Chelsea FC in 1905. Chelsea had a remarkably successful first season and by 1907 their promotion to the First Division saw them attracting the highest gates in the League. Despite staging FA Cup finals and other sporting events, the club did not invest much money in the ground. It was not until 1935 that a cover was added to the Fulham Road Terrace. This was the same year the club recorded its highest ever gate of 82,905 in a game against Arsenal. In 1939 a 2,500-seater stand was erected on the north-east corner, on stilts above the terracing. A new North Stand was opened in 1945, but it was the 1960s and 1970s when major development took place at the Bridge. At the time the West Stand was built, the team were going through one of their most successful periods ever, winning the League Cup in 1965 and the FA Cup in 1970. They also won the European Cup Winners' Cup in 1971. In that year plans were drawn up for the three-tier East Stand, the first stand in the £5.5m development. The stand opened in 1974 but Chelsea's luck took a turn for the worse. They were heavily in debt, they were relegated to the Second Division and gates were dropping. In the 1982/83 season gates twice dropped to below 7,000. It was in this season that Ken Bates took over as chairman. Over the following 20 years, Chelsea Village was developed. Two new all-seater stands were built at each end and corner stands were added. In 2001 the West Stand was rebuilt, a two-tiered stand bringing the capacity up to 42,449.

GROUND: **Stamford Bridge**
ADDRESS: **Stamford Bridge, Fulham Road, London SW6 1HS**
MAIN TEL: **0871 984 1905**
BOX OFFICE: **0871 984 1905**
WEBSITE: **www.chelseafc.com**
CAPACITY: **42,449**
HOME COLOURS: **royal blue shirts with white and amber trim, royal blue shorts with white and blue trim, white socks with blue and amber trim**
CLUB NICKNAME: **the Blues**
PITCH DIMENSIONS: **103m x 68m (113 x 74 yards)**
FOUNDED: **1905**
RECORD ATTENDANCE: **82,905 vs Arsenal, October 12 1935**
MOST PROLIFIC SCORER: **Bobby Tambling (164)**
RECORD WIN: **13-0 vs Jeunesse Hautcharage, September 29 1971**
RECORD DEFEAT: **1-8 vs Wolverhampton Wanderers, December 26 1953**

CRYSTAL PALACE

Crystal Palace was formed in 1905, when the club took up residence at the Crystal Palace ground, which was then England's national stadium. In 1915 the team moved to the Herne Hill cycle and athletics ground as the Admiralty took over its ground. In 1918 Palace moved to the Nest, a ground situated opposite Selhurst station. In 1919 Crystal Palace paid £2,570 for a former brickfield, Selhurst Park. It took a further five years for the site to be prepared. The club's plans for development were fairly conservative, with one stand and minimal terracing. The Main Stand was built to a similar design to those at Chelsea and Fulham. A healthy rise in gates followed its opening, despite the club being relegated. In the 1950s the ground fell into a state of disrepair as the Eagles languished in the Third and Fourth Divisions. The 1960s were more successful. Following the installation of floodlights in 1962, chairman Arthur Wait persuaded Real Madrid to play a friendly at Selhurst Park. The uncovered Park Side was developed in 1969 into a stand with a 42m deep shed-like roof covering the original banking. In 1979 a record 51,482 saw Palace win the Second Division championship. Palace spent the next 12 seasons yo-yoing between the First and Third Divisions. The 1980s also signalled the first ever long-term ground-sharing plans at Selhurst Park, firstly with local rivals Charlton Athletic and then with Wimbledon. The 1990s saw more major development: the Arthur Wait Stand was converted to an all-seater, a hospitality block was built behind the Main Stand and the Whitehorse Lane Stand was developed. The most significant development, however, came at the Holmesdale Road Stand. Built into a natural embankment and surrounded by houses, building work was always going to be difficult. However, structural engineers worked their magic and a massive structure, which took more than a year to build, was finally opened in August 1995, raising the capacity to 26,309.

GROUND: **Selhurst Park**
ADDRESS: **Selhurst Park, Whitehorse Lane, London SE25 6PU**
MAIN TEL: **020 8768 6000**
BOX OFFICE: **0871 200 0071**
WEBSITE: **www.cpfc.co.uk**
CAPACITY: **26,309**
HOME COLOURS: **red and blue striped shirts, red shorts, red socks with blue tops**
CLUB NICKNAMES: **the Eagles, Palace**
PITCH DIMENSIONS: **101m x 68m (110 x 74 yards)**
FOUNDED: **1905**
RECORD ATTENDANCE: **51,482 vs Burnley, May 11 1979**
MOST PROLIFIC SCORER: **Peter Simpson (153)**
RECORD WIN: **9-0 vs Barrow, October 11 1959**
RECORD DEFEAT: **0-9 vs Burnley, February 10 1909**

DERBY COUNTY

Players from Derby County Cricket Club formed Derby County FC in 1884. Their first pitch was part of the cricket ground, which was in the middle of a racecourse. Derby quickly tired of rescheduling games that clashed with race meetings, and in 1895 they moved to a baseball ground that owner Francis Ley had built after a visit to the US. The Baseball Ground, as the stadium became known, was very enclosed however, and in 1923 Derby received an offer to move to Osmanton Park stadium. They turned this offer down and in 1924 they bought the Baseball Ground from Francis Ley. In 1925 the Popular Side was concreted, a year later the Rams went back up to the First Division, which funded further ground developments. A two-tiered stand was built where the Osmanton Terrace and Catcher's Corner had stood, which opened in 1933. By the start of WWII all four sides of the Baseball Ground had been rebuilt and covered. The Rams returned to the First Division in 1969 under the management of Brian Clough; this was the same year the Ley Stand opened, and a record 41,826 fans crammed in to see Derby take on Spurs. Crowd trouble in the late 1970s and 1980s saw fences and bars erected throughout the ground, and calls by local residents for the club to move. In the 1980s the club was struggling under massive debts and they were relegated to the Third Division. These problems were eased when Robert Maxwell took over as chairman in 1984. The fences came down in 1989 and after the Taylor report the club put together plans for rebuilding the stadium. The club were offered another chance to move from the ground, this time to Pride Park. Yet again they turned the offer down and began working on plans for a 28,000 all-seater Baseball Ground. However, in 1995, after seeing the success of Middlesbrough's relocation they moved to Pride Park. The £16m project took 46 weeks to complete and at the start of the 1997/98 season the Rams began playing at Pride Park, a 33,597 all-seater stadium.

GROUND: **Pride Park**
ADDRESS: **Pride Park Stadium, Derby DE24 8XL**
MAIN TEL: **0871 472 1884**
BOX OFFICE: **0871 472 1884**
WEBSITE: **www.dcfc.co.uk**
CAPACITY: **33,597**
HOME COLOURS: **white shirts with black trim, black shorts with white trim, white socks**
CLUB NICKNAME: **the Rams**
PITCH DIMENSIONS: **105m x 68m (115 x 74 yards)**
FOUNDED: **1884**
RECORD ATTENDANCE: **33,597 England vs Mexico, May 25 2001**
MOST PROLIFIC SCORER: **Steve Bloomer (292)**
RECORD WIN: **9-0 vs Wolverhampton Wanderers, January 10 1891**
RECORD DEFEAT: **2-11 vs Everton, January 18 1889**

EVERTON

Everton began as St Domingo's FC in 1878, playing games at Stanley Park. In 1884 the club became the first tenants at Anfield, by which time they had changed their name to Everton. A row with their landlord in 1892 prompted them to move to Goodison Park, then called Mere Green. In 1888 the club became founder members of the League, winning the League title in 1891. Everton spent a great deal of money preparing the ground, building two uncovered stands and a third covered stand with seating, as well as improving the pitch. Mere Green was renamed Goodison Park in time for its official opening in 1892. Everton's support was unrivalled at the time, and the FA was so impressed with the ground they allowed the 1894 Cup Final to be played there. In 1895 the Bullens Road Stand was built following the ground's first international. The Goodison Road Terrace was covered, and by 1905 the ground was estimated to have a capacity of 55,000. In 1907 Scottish engineer Archibald Leitch built the two-tiered Park End Stand at Goodison, before building the magnificent Main Stand in 1909, which had a pitched roof and central gable. It was not until 1926 that the ground saw any more improvements, when a two-tiered stand was built on the Bullens Road side. Twelve years later this was linked to the Gladwys Street end, making Goodison Park the first to have two-tiered stands on all sides. In 1948 the ground saw a record 78,299 fans cram in for a Merseyside derby against Liverpool. In the 1970s the new three-tier Main Stand replaced Leitch's original and a new roof on the Bullen's Road Stand, which was brought round to cover the Gladwys Street end in 1986. In the aftermath of the Taylor report, seats were added to the remaining terraces, and in 1994 the new single-tier Park End Stand was built. There is now talk that the club will move to a new 55,000 purpose-built stadium at Kirkby, as Goodison Park's capacity remains at 40,569.

GROUND: **Goodison Park**
ADDRESS: **Goodison Park, Liverpool L4 4EL**
MAIN TEL: **0870 442 1878**
BOX OFFICE: **0870 442 1878**
WEBSITE: **www.evertonfc.com**
CAPACITY: **40,569**
HOME COLOURS: **royal blue shirts with white trim, white shorts, blue socks**
CLUB NICKNAME: **the Toffees**
PITCH DIMENSIONS: **102m x 71m (112 x 78 yards)**
FOUNDED: **1878**
RECORD ATTENDANCE: **78,299 vs Liverpool, September 18 1948**
MOST PROLIFIC SCORER: **Dixie Dean (349)**
RECORD WIN: **11-2 vs Derby County, January 18 1890**
RECORD DEFEAT: **4-10 vs Tottenham Hotspur, October 11 1958**

GROUND: Craven Cottage
ADDRESS: Craven Cottage, Stevenage Road, London SW6 6HH
MAIN TEL: 0870 442 1222
BOX OFFICE: 0870 442 1234
WEBSITE: www.fulhamfc.com
CAPACITY: 26,300
HOME COLOURS: white shirts with black and red trim, black shorts, white socks with red and black trim
CLUB NICKNAMES: the Cottagers, the Whites
PITCH DIMENSIONS: 102m x 66m (112 x 72 yards)
FOUNDED: 1879
RECORD ATTENDANCE: 49,335 vs Millwall, October 8 1938
MOST PROLIFIC SCORER: Gordon Davies (159)
RECORD WIN: 10-1 vs Ipswich, December 26 1963
RECORD DEFEAT: 0-10 vs Liverpool, September 23 1986

Fulham started in 1879 as Fulham St Andrews, a church team. The club moved grounds eight times before they finally arrived at Craven Cottage in 1896. The ground was on the site of the original Craven Cottage which was built in 1789 by Baron Craven and burned down in 1888. The team turned professional in 1898 and by 1905 they were drawing crowds in the region of 20,000, more than their neighbours at Chelsea. The club spent £15,000 developing the ground; this included three terraces and a corner pavilion, the Cottage. The only stand to be built was on Stevenage Road, which had an upper tier of seats, a paddock in front covered by a pitched roof and gable in the centre. It was not until the 1960s that further development took place. In 1961 the Hammersmith End was extended and in 1965 it was covered. The Riverside Terrace was replaced by the Riverside Stand in 1971, although the cost of this stand almost bankrupted the club. For the next 20 years Fulham fell into decline, gates dropped and debts stacked up. In the early 1990s the club's future at Craven Cottage looked very doubtful as property developers took over ownership of the ground. In 1991 Fulham started ground-sharing talks with Chelsea, although these never came to anything. Perhaps Fulham's lowest moment came in January 1996 when they were second from bottom in the Third Division, drawing crowds of around 4,000 and facing an exit from the League. Their fortunes changed completely on May 29 1997 when Harrod's owner Mohammed Al Fayed took over ownership of the club. Al Fayed brought with him a five-year plan to get the club into the Premiership. He spent millions on players and in just four years this dream was realised. He then went about redeveloping the ground. In 2002 Fulham left Craven Cottage to ground-share at QPR's Loftus Road. Rumours circulated that Al Fayed was going to sell the ground. However these proved unfounded and at the start of the 2004/5 season the Cottagers moved back to Craven Cottage, to an improved stadium, capable of holding 26,300.

HAMPDEN PARK (QUEEN'S PARK)

GROUND: **Hampden Park**
ADDRESS: Hampden Park, Mount Florida, Glasgow, G42 9BA
MAIN TEL AND BOX OFFICE FOR QUEEN'S PARK: 0141 632 1275
MAIN TEL AND BOX OFFICE FOR INTERNATIONALS: 0141 616 6000
WEBSITE: www.queensparkfc.co.uk
www.hampdenpark.co.uk
CAPACITY: 52,000
HOME COLOURS: black and white hooped shirts, white shorts, black socks
CLUB NICKNAME: the Spiders
PITCH DIMENSIONS: 105m x 69m (115 x 75 yards)
FOUNDED: 1867
RECORD CLUB ATTENDANCE: 95,772 vs Rangers, January 12 1929
RECORD HOME INTERNATIONAL ATTENDANCE: 149,415 vs England, April 17 1937
MOST PROLIFIC SCORER: James McAlpine (163)
RECORD WIN: 16-0 vs St Peter's, August 29 1885
RECORD DEFEAT: 0-9 vs Motherwell, April 29 1930

Queen's Park is Scotland's oldest football club, dating back to 1867. The club played early games at Queen's Park Recreation Ground before moving to their own ground, the first Hampden Park on Queen's Drive, in 1873. They moved to Titwood Park in 1883 before moving again to the second Hampden Park in 1884. It was not long before the ground was being used for Scottish FA Cup finals. The club moved again in 1903 to a yet larger site, the third Hampden Park, which had a capacity of 65,000. Scottish architect Archibald Leitch designed the ground's two stands on the south side with a pavilion in between and an oval bowl of terracing around the rest of the ground. The club continued to do well, finishing fifth in the Scottish First Division in 1929. Further development took place in the 1930s when the North Stand was built at the back of the Main Stand terracing, bringing the capacity up to 150,000. This led to the ground being used for internationals and in 1937 the highest crowd ever to attend a football game – 149,415 fans – packed in to see Scotland play England. Until the 1950s Hampden Park was the largest ground in the world. In the 1960s a roof was added to the West Stand, but the club lacked funds to carry out more major, and necessary, refurbishments. During the 1970s Hampden Park's future hung in the balance as the Scottish FA tried to decide how the renovations would be funded. By 1981 an appeal had raised the necessary funds to begin redeveloping Hampden Park. The North Stand was demolished and concrete added to the terraces. The next phase was delayed as the Taylor report meant development was going to be more costly and key thinkers began to question whether it was cost effective to renovate the ground since Ibrox and Murrayfield were so close by. However, eventually a decision was made to develop Hampden Park and in 1992 work began. Seats and roofs were added to the North and East Stands, and now the ground has a 52,000 all-seater capacity. Queen's Park remains the only amateur football club still in the Scottish League.

HEART OF MIDLOTHIAN

Heart of Midlothian FC formed in 1874, taking their name from a dance club in Edinburgh. The club started out playing games on the East Meadows and Powderhall grounds before moving to Gorgie Road in 1881. They moved from the first Tynecastle Park across the road to the current Tynecastle Park in 1886. Hearts was a founder member of the Scottish Football League in 1890. In 1903 a pavilion, a stand and a cycle track were installed. By 1914 Hearts had won two League titles and four Cup finals and they began building a main stand. This came complete with an owl on top to frighten off other birds from the ground. In 1926 the club bought the ground and began building up the terraces, although its location between narrow streets, a school and the North British Distillery meant expansion was going to be very difficult. When a record 53,396 fans crammed in for a Cup tie with Rangers the club seriously thought about relocating to Murrayfield; however, WWII put paid to this plan. The 1950s and '60s saw further successes on the pitch, Hearts won the League twice, the League Cup four times and the Scottish Cup once, all of which helped to fund the concreting of the

terraces and a roof on the Wheatfield Street side. Further development came in the wake of the Safety of Sports Ground Act in the 1970s. Hearts' chairman Walter Mercer ploughed £500,000 into developing the ground, adding benches beneath the Wheatfield Street side plus cover and seats to the Main Stand paddock. The Taylor report led Hearts to consider leaving Tynecastle Park as capacity was so limited. In the end, the club decided to redevelop Tynecastle Park. Two all-seater stands were built on the north and west sides in the mid-1990s, followed by a new stand on the south side. The club's financial worries continue to haunt them and there are still plans for the club to move to Murrayfield if their finances do not improve.

GROUND: **Tynecastle Stadium**
ADDRESS: Tynecastle Stadium, McLeod Street, Edinburgh EH11 2HL
MAIN TEL: 0871 663 1874
BOX OFFICE: 0871 663 1874
WEBSITE: www.heartsfc.co.uk
CAPACITY: 18,008
HOME COLOURS: maroon shirts with white trim, white shorts with maroon trim, maroon socks
CLUB NICKNAME: Hearts, the Jam Tarts
PITCH DIMENSIONS: 98m x 68m (107 x 74 yards)
FOUNDED: 1874
RECORD ATTENDANCE: 53,396 vs Rangers, February 13 1932
MOST PROLIFIC SCORER: John Robertson (208)
RECORD WIN: 10-3 vs Queens Park, August 24 1912
RECORD DEFEAT: 0-7 vs Hibernian, January 1 1973

HIBERNIAN

Hibernian was formed in 1875 by a group of Irish football enthusiasts. They called the team Hibernian after the Latin name for Ireland. At first they shared a ground with Hearts, then moved three times before arriving at the first Easter Road in 1880, not far from their present ground. In 1891 Hibs disbanded after many of their players left to play for Celtic and developers took over the ground. Two years later they re-formed and found themselves a ground not far from the original Easter Road, which opened in February 1893. Success followed and Hibs won their first League title in 1903. There was talk of the club moving again, but in 1922 they signed a 25-year lease on Easter Road. Development began in 1924, when the pitch was moved sideways, raised banking was built on three sides and a stand on the west side. In 1950, Easter Road recorded its highest ever attendance of 65,480 for a game against Hearts and the East Terrace was extended not long afterwards. The North Terrace was covered in the 1960s but no further development came until the 1980s. Easter Road was the first Scottish club to instal undersoil heating in 1980; two years later benches were added to the North Stand and in 1985 the height of the East Terrace was reduced. Hibs was floated on the Stock Exchange and shortly afterwards a business plan was put forward which proposed merger with Hearts to form Edinburgh United. Protests from the fans and investment from chairman David Duff saw off the idea. The Taylor report meant the club had to consider either moving or further developing Easter Road. Plans to

GROUND: **Easter Road Stadium**
ADDRESS: Easter Road Stadium, 12 Albion Place, Edinburgh EH7 5QG
MAIN TEL: 0131 661 2159
BOX OFFICE: 0131 661 1875
WEBSITE: www.hibs.org.uk
CAPACITY: 17,500
HOME COLOURS: green and white shirts, white shorts, green socks with white trim
CLUB NICKNAME: the Hibees
PITCH DIMENSIONS: 102m x 68m (112 x 74 yards)
FOUNDED: 1875
RECORD ATTENDANCE: 65,860 vs Hearts, January 2 1950
MOST PROLIFIC SCORER: Gordon Smith (364)
RECORD WIN: 22-1 vs 42nd Highlanders, September 3 1881
RECORD DEFEAT: 0-6 vs Celtic, October 15 1960

move four miles away to a 20,000 all-seater ground in Straiton were shelved in 1994 following fierce opposition from fans, so Easter Road had to be quickly developed. Two new stands were built at either end and in 2001 a double-decker stand opened on the west side. Seats have been added to the old East Terrace and capacity is now 17,500.

GROUND: **Portman Road**
ADDRESS: Portman Road, Ipswich, Suffolk IP1 2DA
MAIN TEL: 01473 400 500
BOX OFFICE: 0870 111 0555
WEBSITE: www.itfc.co.uk
CAPACITY: 30,300
HOME COLOURS: blue shirts, white shorts, blue socks

CLUB NICKNAMES: the Blues, Town, the Tractor Boys
PITCH DIMENSIONS: 102m x 64 (112 x 70 yards)
FOUNDED: 1878
RECORD ATTENDANCE: 38,010 vs Leeds United, March 8 1975
MOST PROLIFIC SCORER: Ray Crawford (203)
RECORD WIN: 10-0 vs Floriana, September 25 1962
RECORD DEFEAT: 1-10 vs Fulham, December 26 1963

IPSWICH TOWN

Ipswich started as Ipswich AFC in 1878. The club's first ground was on Broom Hill, Norwich Road. In 1888 the football team merged with the local rugby team to become Ipswich Town and they moved to Portman Road, the town's best sporting venue. The rugby team broke away in 1893 but Town continued to share Portman Road with East Suffolk Cricket Club. In 1905 the Ipswich Cricket, Football and Athletic Ground Company formed to pay for separate football and cricket pitches. There was a wooden stand along the Portman Road side but nothing else divided the two pitches. Portman Road suffered when the army took over the ground during WWI. They refused to leave the ground until 1920, by which time the pitch was ruined. Town eventually turned professional in 1936 but the ground still only had one stand. That summer the club put up fencing and terracing, raising the capacity to 15,000. The following year more terracing was added to the Churchman's End and the club added more seats to the East Stand, both of which were further expanded the next season when Ipswich joined the League in 1939. After WWII the supporters club raised virtually all the money needed to fund improvements until 1965. In 1957, under the management of Alf Ramsay, Ipswich was promoted to Division Two. On the basis of this success the club constructed the West Stand, a two-tier stand with a pitched roof. Between 1972-82 Ipswich continued their footballing successes under Bobby Robson, and the Blues carried out extensive redevelopment, replacing the East Stand with the Portman Stand. The next major changes took place in the 1980s when the West Stand was extended and renamed the Pioneer Stand. This stand had to be developed just eight years later following the Taylor report when seats were added. Next, seats were installed on both terraces, and in fact Portman Road was the first Premier League ground to become all-seater. The development continued and the Greene King, or South Stand, opened in 2001, and a year later the new North Stand was opened, bringing the capacity up to 30,300.

LEEDS UNITED

The club started life in 1904 as Leeds City FC. Their ground at Elland Road was originally a grass field, known as the Old Peacock ground, owned by Holbeck Rugby Club. In 1905 Leeds City built the West Stand and that year more than 22,000 fans saw Leeds City play local rivals Bradford City. During the First World War the army used Elland Road for drilling and shooting practice. Leeds United re-formed in 1920 from the remnants of Leeds City, which was disbanded after the club was accused of making illegal payments to players. During the 1920s the development of the ground continued with the erection of the so-called Scratching Shed and the Spion Kop. The most impressive transformations came during the late 1960s, however, in the Don Revie era when support reached record levels. In March 1967 Elland Road saw its highest ever crowd of 57,892 as United battled with Sunderland in the FA Cup. The money the team brought in funded the building of the new Kop in 1968, the season Leeds first became First Division champions. The Scratching Shed was replaced by the South Stand in 1974. Leeds' performances began to falter. Revie believed the ground held bad omens and in 1971 he brought in a gypsy to lift the curse. Revie's theory apparently worked and Leeds won the FA Cup the following year (1972) and became Division One champions in 1973/4. Hooliganism

blighted the club in the '70s and '80s and Elland Road became the first club in the country to instal a police compound to hold troublemakers. The East Stand was the last to be completed in 1992/3, the year after Leeds once again won the First Division championship. Now Elland Road boasts the biggest cantilevered stand in the world.

GROUND: **Elland Road**
ADDRESS: Elland Road, Leeds LS11 0ES
MAIN TEL: 0113 367 6000
BOX OFFICE: 0845 121 1992
WEBSITE: www.leedsunited.com
CAPACITY: 40,204
HOME COLOURS: white shirts, white shorts, white socks
CLUB NICKNAME: United, the Whites, the Peacocks
PITCH DIMENSIONS: 106m x 68m (117 x 76 yards)
FOUNDED: Leeds City 1904; Leeds United 1920
RECORD ATTENDANCE: 57,892 vs Sunderland, March 15 1967
MOST PROLIFIC SCORER: John Charles (153 goals)
RECORD WIN: 8-0 vs Leicester City, April 7 1934
RECORD DEFEAT: 1-8 vs Stoke City, August 27 1934

LEICESTER CITY

Leicester City started in 1884 as Leicester Fosse as many of the team's founder members lived near Fosse Way in the city's west end. In their first year they played at the racecourse before moving the following year to Victoria Park. In 1889 Leicester turned professional and moved to Mill Lane, which they left two years later when they found Filbert Street. While the Filbert Street site was being prepared for football, the team played home games at Aylestone Road Cricket Ground. Filbert Street was known then as Walnut Street and the facilities included a low main stand. It wasn't until after WWI that Leicester began their major development of the ground and changed their name to Leicester City. In 1921 the new Main Stand was opened, coming complete with mock classical podium and a very grand players' entrance to the pitch with a small window either side of the players' tunnel and brass rails. In 1927 the club built a two-tier stand at the Kop End, and moved the Kop to the Filbert Street End. In February 1928, 47,298 fans crammed in to see the Foxes take on Spurs in the FA Cup, the largest crowd ever at Filbert Street. In the late 1930s the last remaining open section was covered. The next phase of major development was in the 1970s, when the club began converting terraces to seating. The development started in 1971 with the Filbert Street Terrace, which became the North Stand; next the Popular Side was turned into the all-seater East Stand. The 1990s saw further plans for change, and the club considered either building a completely new stand, or turning the pitch 90°. In the end they opted to do neither and rebuilt the Main Stand. However, this was not enough and in 2002 they moved to the all-seater Walkers Stadium. At a cost of £35m, the new stadium is completely enclosed, with all sides the same height and style.

GROUND: **Walkers Stadium**
ADDRESS: Filbert Way, Leicester LE2 7FL
MAIN TEL: 0844 815 6000
BOX OFFICE: 0844 815 5000
WEBSITE: www.lcfc.co.uk
CAPACITY: 32,500
HOME COLOURS: blue shirts, white shorts, blue socks
CLUB NICKNAME: the Foxes, the Filberts
PITCH DIMENSIONS: 101m x 69m (110 x 76 yards)
FOUNDED: 1884
RECORD ATTENDANCE: 32,148 vs Newcastle United, December 26 2003
MOST PROLIFIC SCORER: Arthur Chandler (259)
RECORD WIN: 10-0 vs Portsmouth, October 10 1928
RECORD DEFEAT: 0-12 vs Nottingham Forest, April 21 1909

LIVERPOOL

GROUND: Anfield

ADDRESS: Anfield Road, Liverpool L4 0TH
MAIN TEL: 0151 263 2361
BOX OFFICE: 0870 220 2345
WEBSITE: www.liverpoolfc.tv
CAPACITY: 45,362
HOME COLOURS: red shirts, red shorts, red socks
CLUB NICKNAME: the Reds, Pool
PITCH DIMENSIONS: 101m x 69m (110 x 75 yards)
FOUNDED: 1892
RECORD ATTENDANCE: 61,905 vs Wolverhampton Wanderers, February 2 1952
MOST PROLIFIC SCORER: Roger Hunt (245)
RECORD WIN: 10-1 vs Rotherham Town, February 18 1896
RECORD DEFEAT: 1-9 vs Birmingham City, December 11 1954

Anfield was originally home to Everton, who played there from 1884 until 1892, when they had a disagreement with Anfield's owner John Houlding and moved on to Goodison Park. Houlding set up his own team, Liverpool, which was dominated by Scottish players. Major changes took place at Anfield in 1906, the season Liverpool won their second League title. The pitch was raised by five feet and in addition to the two existing covered sides, a new main stand and south terrace were built. The Kop was one of the tallest terraces in England, complete with 50ft flagpole, and was covered in 1928 when it became Britain's largest covered terrace, with a capacity of 28,000. During the era of Bill Shankley in the 1960s, Liverpool carried out further renovations to the ground. The Kemlyn Road Stand was rebuilt and reopened in 1964, the same season that Liverpool won their first FA Cup final. The 1970s saw the Main Stand extended, and the club began buying houses along Kemlyn Road so they could build a second tier on the Kemlyn Road Stand. It wasn't until 1990 when the final residents – two elderly sisters – agreed to sell up. April 15 1989 is a day that will forever remain in the memories of Liverpool fans, the date of the Hillsborough disaster, when 96 Liverpool fans were crushed to death. The resulting Taylor report had a massive impact on football grounds across the country. At Anfield plans were drawn up to make the Kop all-seater, so that a tragedy on the scale of Hillsborough could never happen again. It was a sad day for many fans in 1994 when the Kop was finally demolished. Liverpool has now announced plans to move to nearby Stanley Park, to a purpose-built 60,000 all-seater stadium. The strong ties many fans feel to Anfield means this move is deeply unpopular with some.

MANCHESTER CITY

GROUND: City of Manchester Stadium
ADDRESS: City of Manchester Stadium, Sportcity, Rowsley Street, Manchester M11 3FF
MAIN TEL: 0161 231 3200
BOX OFFICE: 0870 062 1894
WEBSITE: www.mcfc.co.uk
CAPACITY: 48,000
HOME COLOURS: sky blue shirts, white shorts, navy socks
CLUB NICKNAME: the Blues, the Citizens
PITCH DIMENSIONS: 107m x 71m (117 x 78 yards)
FOUNDED: 1887
RECORD ATTENDANCE: 47,321 vs Liverpool, December 30 2007
MOST PROLIFIC SCORER: Tommy Johnson (158)
RECORD WIN: 10-1 vs Huddersfield, November 7 1987
RECORD DEFEAT: 1-9 vs Everton, September 3 1906

anchester City's roots go back to an amalgamation between local teams West orton and Gorton Athletic in 1887. At first the club played as Ardwick, before anging their name to Manchester City in 1894. They played games on Hyde Road, a nall ground penned in by a railway line and houses, but it had two stands, paid for th the help of a local brewery. When, in 1920, the Main Stand burned down, the ub decided it was time to move. At the start of the 1923 season the club opened e doors to their new home at Maine Road. The ground was vast; in the 1920s it d a capacity in excess of 80,000 and regular gates of 37,000, the highest gates in e League. In 1934, 84,569 fans turned out to see City take on Stoke in the Cup. llowing WWII local rivals Manchester United became lodgers at Maine Road and ofits soared. The Blues spent some of this money on wooden benches, which were stalled under the Platt Lane roof in the 1950s. In 1956 City won their third FA Cup d built a roof over the Kippax Terrace, leaving just the Scoreboard End uncovered. is end was replaced by the North Stand in 1971. In 1983 the club replaced the of on the Main Stand. Following the Taylor report, in 1992 the Platt Lane Stand as demolished and replaced by the Umbro Stand, which cost City £5m and plunged e club into debt. The report's requirements meant the club had to demolish the

Kippax Terrace and replace it with an all-seater stand. The new stand cost £11m and brought Maine Road's capacity up to 32,344. Despite spending £19m on developments, in 2003 the club left Maine Road and became tenants of the brand new City of Manchester Stadium, built for the 2002 Commonwealth Games. The club spent £20m turning the athletics stadium into a football ground, expanding the stands and bringing them closer to the pitch. The bowl-shaped stadium has a capacity of 48,000 and is totally enclosed by two three-tiered stands and two two-tiered stands.

MANCHESTER UNITED

Manchester United began life in 1878 when it was formed by railway workers from the Lancashire and Yorkshire Railway. It was known as Newton Heath FC. The Heathens played early matches on North Road, before moving to Bank Street, Clayton in 1893, a year after joining the League. By 1902 their debts had grown so large they went into liquidation. Local brewer John H Davies rescued the club and changed their name to Manchester United. The club's fortunes on the pitch also changed; by 1906 they were back in the First Division and had cover on all sides of the ground, a main stand with a gallery and a total capacity of 50,000. In 1908 United won their first League title and the FA Cup in 1909. A year later the club said farewell to Bank Street and moved five miles away to a new ground at Old Trafford. By then Davies had invested £60,000 and had developed the ground into a rectangle with curved corners and a multi-span main stand. In 1931 United were relegated, crowds dropped to 3,500 and the club faced bankruptcy for the second time. Up stepped James Gibson, a wealthy businessman, who cleared the club's debts and funded a cover over the United Road side. The ground was badly damaged during the WWII and United began ground-sharing with Manchester City. It was not until 1949 that Old Trafford was repaired and United returned. The pitched roof covering the south-west corner was expanded to cover the Stretford End in 1959, the year after the Munich air crash. The 1960s saw further development at the ground, when Old Trafford was selected as a venue for World Cup games. In 1965 they built a new two-tier stand over the United Road Terrace capable of seating 10,000 and holding a further 10,000 standing. This new stand also held the first executive boxes at a European football ground. From then until the 1990s United gradually converted Old Trafford into a fully enclosed all-seater stadium. New plans to expand capacity were drawn up in 1995. A three-tiered North Stand opened in 1996 and second tiers were added to the East and West Stands in 2001. In 2006 north-east and north-west quadrants were opened bringing the capacity to 76,100.

GROUND: **Old Trafford**
ADDRESS: **Sir Matt Busby Way, Old Trafford. Manchester M16 0RA**
MAIN TEL: **0870 442 1994**
BOX OFFICE: **0870 442 1999**
WEBSITE: **www.manutd.com**
CAPACITY: **76,100**
HOME COLOURS: **red shirts, white shorts, black socks**
CLUB NICKNAME: **the red Devils**
PITCH DIMENSIONS: **106m x 69m (116 x 76 yards)**
FOUNDED: **1878**
RECORD ATTENDANCE: **76,962 Wolves vs Grimsby, FA Cup semi-final, March 25 1939**
MOST PROLIFIC SCORER: **Bobby Charlton (199)**
RECORD WIN: **10-0 vs Anderlecht, September 26 1956**
RECORD DEFEAT: **0-7 vs Blackburn Rovers, April 10 1926**

MIDDLESBROUGH

Middlesbrough formed in 1876, although the club didn't find themselves a proper home until 1879, when they moved to Breckon Hill Road and again a year later to Middlesbrough Cricket Club, Linthorpe Road. At Linthorpe Road the club built a small stand and in 1899 Boro joined the League. By 1902 it was clear the ground was too small and in 1903 they moved to Ayresome Park. The Scottish architect Archibald Leitch helped the club in its mission to prepare the ground and build a stadium in nine months. He designed a two-tier stand with a semi-circular gable and barrel roof, capable of seating 2,000, and incorporated the old stand from Linthorpe Road into the stadium together with banking at both ends. The next major development came in the 1930s when the South Stand was replaced by a two-tier stand and the West End was given a roof. After the war the club made further improvements to the terracing and in 1949 the ground held a record 53,596 fans as Boro took on Newcastle. Ayresome Park was selected as a venue for some of the

1966 World Cup matches, and the club undertook a number of major ground improvements, including adding a roof to the East End and seats to the North, South and East Terraces. In the following years Middlesbrough's success faltered and support dwindled. In 1986 fire safety checks revealed the ground needed significant attention. Due to Middlesbrough's huge debts, the club was unable to carry out repairs and had to play home games at Hartlepool. The ground had £800,000 spent on it following the Taylor report: fences were removed, seats installed in the South and East Stands and plans made to redevelop the North Stand. However, in 1994 self-made millionaire Steve Gibson took over a 68 per cent share in the club and in April 1995 Boro played their last game at Ayresome Park. At a cost of £12m, the club have now moved to the site of a former petro-chemical storage facility. The two-tiered West Stand and the single tiers on the other three sides totally enclose the new 35,100-seater stadium.

GROUND: **Riverside Stadium**
ADDRESS: Riverside Stadium, Middlesbrough, Cleveland TS3 6RS
MAIN TEL: 0844 499 6789
BOX OFFICE: 0844 499 1234
WEBSITE: www.mfc.co.uk
CAPACITY: 35,100
HOME COLOURS: red shirts with white trim, red shorts, red socks
CLUB NICKNAME: Boro
PITCH DIMENSIONS: 105m x 69m (115 x 75 yards)
FOUNDED: 1876
RECORD ATTENDANCE: 35,000 England vs Slovakia, June 11 2003
MOST PROLIFIC SCORER: George Camsell (326)
RECORD WIN: 9-0 vs Brighton & Hove Albion, August 23 1958
RECORD DEFEAT: 0-9 vs Blackburn Rovers, November 6 1954

MILLENNIUM STADIUM

The Millennium Stadium was opened in October 1999 on the site of Cardiff Arms Park. The ground dates back to the 17th century, but was first called Cardiff Arms Park in 1787. Cricket was the first sport played at the ground from 1848; rugby was played there from 1876. The Grandstand was opened in 1885, a year before football was first played there. An extension to the Grandstand was added in 1890, and a grand pavilion was built in 1904. The Grandstand was replaced by the South Stand in 1912. The Park's owner Lord Bute sold the ground in 1922 and the rugby and cricket clubs set up a joint company to take over the ground. The North Stand opened in 1934 and the South Stand was built in 1956 after Cardiff was selected to stage the 1958 Commonwealth Games. In 1968, the Welsh Rugby Union (WRU) took over Cardiff Arms Park and there followed a 16-year period of redevelopment. A new two-tiered stand was erected in place of the North Stand. The East Terrace opened in 1980, and finally the South Stand opened in 1984. Football returned to Cardiff Arms Park in 1989. Just six years later the WRU decided that the ground's 53,500 capacity was not enough. They submitted plans to the Millennium Commission for an ambitious 75,000-seater stadium to be created on the site of the Park. The Commission stumped up £50

million and the other £114 million was funded by commercial sources. The ground was built in time for the 1999 Rugby World Cup and quickly established itself as a unique sporting venue. The Millennium Stadium has Britain's first retractable roof, and the pitch is grown outside the ground and brought in when needed. It is completely enclosed with curved corners and three tiers on three sides. The North Stand remains a two-tier structure as it backs on to a rugby club, leaving no room for a third tier. Capacity is now 74,500. As well as rugby, the ground now stages play-off finals, British Speedway Grand Prix races and concerts.

GROUND: **Millennium Stadium**
ADDRESS: Millennium Stadium, Westgate Street, Cardiff CF10 1NS
MAIN TEL: 0870 013 8600
BOX OFFICE: 0870 558 2582
WEBSITE: www.millenniumstadium.com
CAPACITY: 74,500
PITCH DIMENSIONS: 101m x 66m (110 yards x 72 yards)
OPENED: 1999
PREVIOUS NAME: Cardiff Arms Park

MILLWALL

Millwall Rovers was formed in 1885 by workers from Morton's Jam factory on the Isle of Dogs. Most of the workers at the factory were Scottish, so the kit was blue and white to reflect the Scottish flag. The club played at four different grounds on the Isle of Dogs and changed their name to Millwall Athletic, before finally relocating south of the river to The Den, Cold Blow Lane, in 1910. When The Den opened, only the Main Stand had been built, with banking on the other three sides. In 1920 Millwall joined League Division Three and dropped "Athletic" from its name. The ground developed during the following decade and saw its highest attendance of 48,672 in an FA Cup tie against Derby County on February 20, 1937. WWII came just when Millwall were forming a strong side. New Cross suffered badly during the Blitz and the Main Stand was severely damaged. With compensation from the War Damages Commission, the club began rebuilding the stands. They covered the Ilderton Road End in 1947 and the two remaining sides during the 1950s. Little changed inside the ground for the next 40 years, except an extension to the Ilderton Road End and seating in the paddock. Millwall played their last game at The Den in 1993, 83 years after arriving. They moved a quarter of a mile away to a new 20,000 all-seater stadium at a cost of £16m, also called The Den. One of the many reasons for this move was the hope that livelier elements of some sections of the Millwall faithful might be tamed by the constrictions of an all-seater stadium. Similar to the old ground, the new ground was designed by Scottish architects and engineers. The Den now consists of four stands which, from inside the stadium, appear almost identical. In fact only the North Stand and Cold Blow Lane End are the same.

GROUND: **The Den**
ADDRESS: **The Den, Zampa Road, London SE16 3LN**
MAIN TEL: **020 7232 1222**
BOX OFFICE: **020 7231 9999**
WEBSITE: **www.millwallfc.co.uk**
CAPACITY: **20,146**
HOME COLOURS: **blue shirt, white shorts, blue socks**
CLUB NICKNAME: **the Lions**
PITCH DIMENSIONS: **96m x 62m (105 x 68 yards)**
FOUNDED: **1885**
RECORD ATTENDANCE: **20,093 vs Arsenal, January 10 1994**
MOST PROLIFIC SCORER: **Teddy Sheringham (93)**
RECORD WIN: **9-1 vs Torquay United, September 29 1927**
RECORD DEFEAT: **1-9 vs Aston Villa, January 28 1946**

NEWCASTLE UNITED

Newcastle United began life as East End FC. The club formed in 1881 and first played at Chillingham Road in Heaton; they moved to St James' Park in 1892. Early facilities were very basic and the pitch had a distinctive slant. Following the club's promotion in 1898, the ground's capacity of 15,000 was severely stretched. The next year an extra four acres were leased to the club, so they relocated the pitch and moved tons of soil to even out the surface. They cut terracing into the banks of the Leazes Park End and Leazes Terrace. In 1905, after losing the FA Cup final but winning the League, Newcastle drew the largest crowds in the League, so they began revamping the stadium. The wooden stands were cleared, three sides of banking were expanded, terraced and wire barriers added. The West Stand was built with seating for 4,680, beneath which was a swimming pool for the players. The ground opened in November 1905 with a new capacity of 65,000. The 1920s saw more improvements, with yet another pitch laid. A new cover was put on the Leazes Park End in 1930 and plans were drawn up to extend the other sides, although the council rejected these. The same year a record crowd of 68,386 fans saw Newcastle take on Chelsea; at this time the average gate was over 56,000. The Magpies had three FA Cup victories between 1951-55, which sent profits soaring, however every attempt to expand the ground was rejected and a feud developed between the club and the council. In 1971 the club were finally granted a 99-year lease on the ground and permission to build a new 3,400-seater stand backing on to Leazes Terrace. The next major development came in 1987 when the 6,607-seater Jackie Milburn Stand was built. Sir John Hall joined the board in 1992, and he took full control of the club in 1994. He spent £23.5m on completely redeveloping St James' Park, with all-seater stands at each end and corner, and additional tiers on the north and west sides and the north-west corner, raising capacity to 52,327.

GROUND: **St James' Park**
ADDRESS: **St James' Park, Newcastle-upon-Tyne NE1 4ST**
MAIN TEL: **0191 201 8400**
BOX OFFICE: **0191 261 1571**
WEBSITE: **www.nufc.co.uk**
CAPACITY: **52,327**
HOME COLOURS: **black and white striped shirts with blue trim, black shorts, black socks with white trim**
CLUB NICKNAMES: **the Magpies, the Toon**
PITCH DIMENSIONS: **101m x 67m (110 x 73 yards)**
FOUNDED: **1881**
RECORD ATTENDANCE: **68,386 vs Chelsea, September 3 1930**
MOST PROLIFIC SCORER: **Alan Shearer (206)**
RECORD WIN: **13-0 vs Newport County, October 5 1946**
RECORD DEFEAT: **0-9 vs Burton Wanderers, April 15 1895**

NORWICH CITY

Football has been played in Norwich since 1868, but Norwich City did not form until 1902. Their first ground on Newmarket Road belonged to the Norfolk County FA. The Canaries turned professional in 1905, yet there were problems with their rented ground. Their chairman John Pyke thought he had solved these when he bought a disused chalk pit on Rosary Road. A wooden stand was brought with the club to the new ground, which labourers spent the summer of 1908 preparing for football. The ground was named the Nest, but it was not a particularly suitable home for the Canaries, as houses were very close to the pitch at the west end and there was a steep concrete verge at the east end. In 1922 barriers on top of the verge collapsed and a boy was badly injured. Despite the problems, the club continued to play on the ground until 1935. That year the club moved to Carrow Road, a sports ground owned by Colman's Mustard. In just 82 days the club built a 3,500-seater main stand and paddock on one side and embankments on the other three sides. In 1937 the first terrace cover went up

at the Station End, renamed the Barclay End, but it was not until 1959, when the Canaries reached the semi-finals of the FA Cup and won promotion, that they could afford further ground improvements. The terrace opposite the Main Stand was covered and in 1963 the South Stand was built. Fire destroyed the central section of the Main Stand in October 1984, which was replaced the following season. The 1990s saw the ground almost completely rebuilt, with new stands on each side. The most recent to be opened is the Jarrold Road South Stand in 2004; this can hold 8,000 fans. There are two-tiered stands at either end and the Geoffrey Watling City Stand is a smaller single-tiered stand.

GROUND: **Carrow Road**
ADDRESS: Carrow Road, Norwich NR1 1JE
MAIN TEL: 01603 760 760
BOX OFFICE: 0870 444 1902
WEBSITE: www.canaries.co.uk
CAPACITY: 26,034
HOME COLOURS: yellow shirts, green shorts, yellow socks
CLUB NICKNAME: the Canaries
PITCH DIMENSIONS: 101m x 69m (114 x 74 yards)
FOUNDED: 1902
RECORD ATTENDANCE: 43,984 vs Leicester City, March 30 1963
MOST PROLIFIC SCORER: Johnny Gavin (122)
RECORD WIN: 10-2 vs Coventry City, March 15 1930
RECORD DEFEAT: 2-10 vs Swindon Town, September 5 1908

NOTTINGHAM FOREST

Nottingham Forest formed in 1865 and played their first games at the Forest Recreation Ground. They moved in 1879 to the Meadows and just a year later moved again to Trent Bridge, the cricket ground. The club then had a number of different homes and it was not until 1890 that Forest settled for a while at the Town Ground. It cost the club £1,000 to prepare the ground for football. Forest joined the League in 1892 and in 1898 they won their first FA Cup final. Their success brought increased numbers of supporters and that year the Reds moved to the City Ground, spending £3,000 getting it up to scratch. The club built a wooden main stand and a wooden shelter at the Trent End. The City Ground survived the war with very little damage – it cost more to repair the ground when the Trent burst its banks in 1947. After winning the Third Division title in 1950 the club drew up plans to redevelop the ground. In 1954 the Trent End Terrace was extended and covered, and three years later the club built the East Stand and expanded the Bridgford End Terrace. Between 1962-65 the Main Stand was redeveloped in time for Forest's highest gate ever when 49,946 fans saw them take on Manchester United in 1967. The following season fire engulfed the Main Stand in a game against Leeds United – fortunately no fans were injured. The club had to move temporarily to Meadow Lane, Notts County's ground, for six games while The City Ground was repaired. The late 1970s saw Forest win the League title, the European Cup and the League Cup twice in successive seasons. The money earned from this success funded the building of the two-tiered, all-seater Executive Stand (now called the Brian Clough Stand) in place of the East Stand, at a cost of a cool £2.5m. After a wrangle with the council over a strip of land behind the Trent End, Forest began developing the Bridgford End in 1992, followed shortly afterwards by the Trent End which brought capacity to 30,602.

GROUND: **The City Ground**
ADDRESS: **The City Ground, Nottingham NG2 5FJ**
MAIN TEL: **0115 982 4444**
BOX OFFICE: **0871 226 1980**
WEBSITE: **www.nottinghamforest.co.uk**
CAPACITY: **30,602**
HOME COLOURS: **red shirts, white shorts with red trim, red socks**
CLUB NICKNAME: **the Reds**
PITCH DIMENSIONS: **105m x 68m (115 x 78 yards)**
FOUNDED: **1865**
RECORD ATTENDANCE: **49,946 vs Manchester United, October 28 1967**
MOST PROLIFIC SCORER: **Grenville Morris (119)**
RECORD WIN: **14-0 vs Clapton, January 17 1891**
RECORD DEFEAT: **1-9 vs Blackburn Rovers, April 10 1937**

PORTSMOUTH

Portsmouth formed in 1898 after the town's other football club, the Royal Artillery, were suspended by the FA for breaching amateur regulations. The club bought land near Fratton railway station and Fratton Park was opened in September 1899. The club progressed well at the start of the 20th century, generating enough money to build a mock-Tudor pavilion at the Frogmore Road entrance complete with clock tower. In 1920 the club joined the League and were soon promoted to Division Two. In 1925 they opened the South Stand, which had 4,000 seats, a paddock and a balcony. Despite losing the 1929 and 1934 Cup finals, their profits continued to rise and they were able to fund the building of the North Stand in 1935. Pompey finally got their hands on the FA Cup in 1939, when they thrashed Wolves 4-1. After WWII, Portsmouth won the League in 1949 and 1950 and were drawing average gates of 39,000. They notched up their largest crowd ever in February 1949 when 51,385 people saw them take on Derby County in the FA Cup. The Fratton End was covered in 1956, but it was not until 1988 that any further development took place at Fratton Park. Jim Gregory bought the club and between 1988/94 funded a £4m refurbishment programme. The Fratton End was demolished in 1988 but plans for the replacement all-seater stand had to be shelved when British Rail refused to sell land behind the ground. In April 1993 the club unveiled plans for a move to Parkway Stadium in Farlington, although these were turned down by Whitehall. In 1995 the ground was partly rebuilt and made all-seater bringing the capacity up to 20,288. Following the club's successful promotion to the Premiership in 2003, ambitious plans have been announced to move to a new high tech stadium at the dockyard.

GROUND: **Fratton Park**
ADDRESS: **Fratton Park, Frogmore Road, Portsmouth PO4 8RA**
MAIN TEL: **023 9273 1204**
BOX OFFICE: **0844 847 1898**
WEBSITE: **www.portsmouthfc.co.uk**
CAPACITY: **20,288**
HOME COLOURS: **blue shirts, white shorts, red socks**
CLUB NICKNAME: **Pompey**
PITCH DIMENSIONS: **105m x 67m (115 x 73 yards)**
FOUNDED: **1898**
RECORD ATTENDANCE: **51,385 vs Derby County, February 26 1949**
MOST PROLIFIC SCORER: **Peter Harris (194)**
RECORD WIN: **9-1 vs Notts County, April 9 1927**
RECORD DEFEAT: **0-10 vs Leicester City, October 20 1928**

RANGERS

Rangers was formed in 1873 and the club played its first games on Glasgow Green. They moved twice before arriving at Ibrox in 1887 to a ground which borders their current ground. The original Ibrox was a success and hosted the 1890 Cup Final and three internationals. However, when local rivals Celtic opened the more sophisticated Celtic Park, Rangers began looking for a grander ground. In 1899, after winning the League without losing a game, Rangers began building on the land next to their pitch. When it opened it boasted an oval track, a pavilion and a stand. In 1900 Scottish architect Archibald Leitch built terracing behind the west goal capable of holding 36,000 fans. However, the terracing was unstable and in a game between England and Scotland in 1902 there was a tragic collapse killing 26 and injuring 500. By 1910 Leitch had again been commissioned to expand Ibrox and increase its capacity to 63,000. Rangers won the League and Cup double in 1928 and this funded the building of the 10,000-seater double-decker South Stand. The Gers continued to enlarge the banking and in 1939 a record 118,567 turned up for an Old Firm derby. Tragedy struck again at Ibrox in 1971, when 66 people died and 145 were injured as the notorious Stairway 13 in the ground's north-east corner collapsed at the end of a game against Celtic. Following the tragedy, the club planned to completely rebuild all sides except for Leitch's South Stand and make the three new stands all-seater. Work began in 1978 and the new Ibrox opened in 1981 at a cost of £10m. However, hard times followed and attendances dropped. Heavy investment in 1986 saw the club's fortunes reverse and in 1988 they spent £4m on the rear of the Govan Stand. Yet more investment came when new chairman David Murray took over; he spent £20m adding another tier to the South Stand, making it all-seater. An innovative move to increase capacity involved the lowering of the pitch by 12 inches, in 1991, and the corners at either side of the Govan stand were also completed in 1996, bringing Ibrox's all-seated capacity up to 50,411.

GROUND: **Ibrox**
ADDRESS: Ibrox Stadium Glasgow, G51 2XD
MAIN TEL: 0871 702 1972
BOX OFFICE: 0871 702 1972
WEBSITE: www.rangers.co.uk
CAPACITY: 50,411
HOME COLOURS: blue, red and white
CLUB NICKNAME: the Gers or Teddy Bears
PITCH DIMENSIONS: 105m x 69m (115 x 78 yards)
FOUNDED: 1873
RECORD ATTENDANCE: 118,567 vs Celtic, January 2 1939
MOST PROLIFIC SCORER: Ally McCoist (355)
RECORD WIN: 13-0 vs Possilpark, October 6 1877
RECORD DEFEAT: 1-7 vs Celtic, October 19 1957

READING

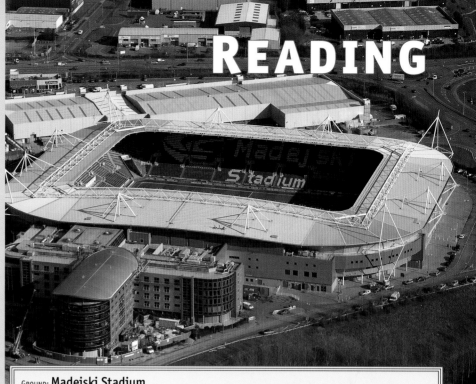

Reading FC was formed in 1871, and played their first games at the Reading Recreation Ground. The club moved several times and eventually settled in Elm Park in 1894. The ground opened in 1896 and had turfed terraces around the pitch and a single wooden main stand on the Norfolk Road side. The club built an L-shaped terrace cover over the north-west corner, although this was blown down in a gale in 1925, as was the Main Stand. In 1926 Reading were preparing to play in the Second Division and so rebuilt the Main Stand. The following year saw Elm Park attract its highest capacity ever, with 33,042 packing in to see a Cup tie against Brentford. A roof was added to the South Bank in 1936, which was extended to cover the Town End and the Tilehurst End by the mid 1950s. Little changed at Elm Park until the 1980s when Robert Maxwell, then chairman of local rivals Oxford United, announced that the two clubs were going to merge into one team. This brought sweeping changes in the Reading boardroom and management and a merger was avoided. A new chairman Roger Smee took over and and despite improving the ground, he started drawing up plans to move the club to a new site, close to the M4. There was widespread support for the plans but there was not the cash available to make them a reality. In 1990 Roger Smee resigned and businessman John Madejski stepped in with much needed cash investment. The Madejski is a totally enclosed stadium with single-tier stands on three sides and a two-tier stand on the west side of the pitch. There are plans to increase capacity at the stadium.

GROUND: **Madejski Stadium**
ADDRESS: **Madejski Stadium, Junction 11, M4, Reading RG2 0FL**
MAIN TEL: **0118 968 1100**
BOX OFFICE: **0870 999 1871**
WEBSITE: **www.readingfc.co.uk**
CAPACITY: **24,200**
HOME COLOURS: **royal blue and white hooped shirts, blue shorts, blue socks with white hoops**
CLUB NICKNAME: **the Royals**

PITCH DIMENSIONS: **102m x 70m (112 x 77 yards)**
FOUNDED: **1871**
RECORD ATTENDANCE: **(at Elm Park) 24,122 vs Aston Villa, February 2007**
RECORD ATTENDANCE: **(at Madejski Stadium) 24,135 vs Manchester United, January 19 2008**
MOST PROLIFIC SCORER: **Ronnie Blackman (158)**
RECORD WIN: **10-2 vs Crystal Palace, September 4 1946**
RECORD DEFEAT: **0-18 vs Preston North End, January 27 1893**

SHEFFIELD UNITED

Sheffield United first played at Bramall Lane in 1862 when Hallam FC took on Sheffield FC, the world's oldest football club. The ground was originally used by Sheffield United Cricket Club from 1854. In 1874 an exhibition baseball match was played at the ground and bowls, lacrosse, cycling, tennis and athletics were also played there. It was not until 1889 that Sheffield United Football Club was formed. Success was rapid; in 1892 they were elected to the Second Division, earning promotion just a year later and winning their only League championship in 1898. Two stands were built at this time, at the Shoreham Street End and on John Street. Glaswegian engineers were behind the 1902 design of the John Street Stand, replacing the earlier one that had been gutted by fire. The Blades won the FA Cup that season for the second time in their history. Just before the First World War terracing was extended along the Bramall Lane End, known to fans as the Kop. A roof was added in 1935 and just a year later Bramall Lane notched up its highest attendance ever, with 68,287 fans (many of whom sat on the roof) cramming in to see the Blades take on Leeds United. Bramall Lane was bombed 10 times during the war, damaging the John Street Stand, the Kop roof and the pitch. It took until 1954 to replace the John Street Stand. The South Stand opened in 1975, at a cost of £1m. The ground had a capacity of 49,000, yet the club's fortunes were faltering. By 1981, the Blades were in the Fourth Division with gates of fewer than 15,000. The 1990s saw a new owner and further development of the ground. The John Street Stand was demolished in 1994 and a new stand opened in 1996. Two of the ground's corners have now been filled bringing the capacity up to 32,609.

GROUND: **Bramall Lane**
ADDRESS: **Bramall Lane, Sheffield S2 4SU**
MAIN TEL: **0871 222 1899**
BOX OFFICE: **0871 222 1899**
WEBSITE: **www.sufc.co.uk**
CAPACITY: **32,609**
HOME COLOURS: **red and white striped shirts, black shorts, red socks**
CLUB NICKNAME: **the Blades**
PITCH DIMENSIONS: **103m x 66m (112 x 72 yards)**
FOUNDED: **1889**
RECORD ATTENDANCE: **68,287 vs Leeds United, February 15 1936**
MOST PROLIFIC SCORER: **Joe Shaw (629)**
RECORD WIN: **10-0 vs Port Vale, December 10 1892**
RECORD DEFEAT: **0-13 vs Bolton Wanderers, February 1 1890**

SHEFFIELD WEDNESDAY

GROUND: Hillsborough
ADDRESS: **Hillsborough, Sheffield S6 1SW**
MAIN TEL: **0870 999 1867**
BOX OFFICE: **0871 230 1867**
WEBSITE: **www.swfc.co.uk**
CAPACITY: **39,814**
HOME COLOURS: **blue and white striped shirts, black shorts, black socks**
CLUB NICKNAME: **the Owls**
PITCH DIMENSIONS: **105m x 69m (115 x 75 yards)**
FOUNDED: **1867**
RECORD ATTENDANCE: **72,841 vs Manchester City, February 17 1934**
MOST PROLIFIC SCORER: **Andy Wilson (199)**
RECORD WIN: **12-0 vs Halliwell, January 17 1891**
RECORD DEFEAT: **0-10 vs Aston Villa, October 5 1912**

Sheffield Wednesday was established in 1867 as the football playing section of Wednesday Cricket Club. The club played at various grounds before severing ties with the cricket club and moving to Olive Grove in 1887. In 1892 the club joined the League and in 1896 won the FA Cup. This success financed the building of the Main Stand. The lease to the ground came up in 1898 and Wednesday found themselves homeless. The supporters were invited to help choose a new ground. None of the selected grounds were suitable and in 1899 the club moved to a ground in Owlerton bringing with them the Main Stand from the Olive Ground. The new ground seemed to bring the club good luck; in 1903 and 1904 they won the League title and in 1907 they won the FA Cup again. It was not until 1913 that further development took place, with the Spion Kop and the South Stand being built. The club changed the ground's name to Hillsborough in 1914 and when the Kop finally opened later that year the capacity was 50,000. In 1927 the Leppings Lane End was expanded, and by 1934 a record 72,841 fans packed in to see the Owls take on Manchester City. A cantilevered grandstand, the North Stand, capable of seating 9,882 fans, replaced the Olive Grove Stand in 1961. Hillsborough was selected as a venue for some of the games in the 1966 World Cup, so Wednesday built the new West Stand and added seats to the South Stand paddock. On April 15 1989 the ground saw its darkest day when 96 Liverpool fans were crushed to death in the Leppings Lane End. This event changed the future of British football and the resulting Taylor report required all top clubs in England, Wales and Scotland to become all-seater by the start of the 1994 season. The Owls spent £10m on ground improvements, adding seats to the South Stand, the lower tier of the West Stand and the Kop. The ground can now hold 39,814.

SOUTHAMPTON

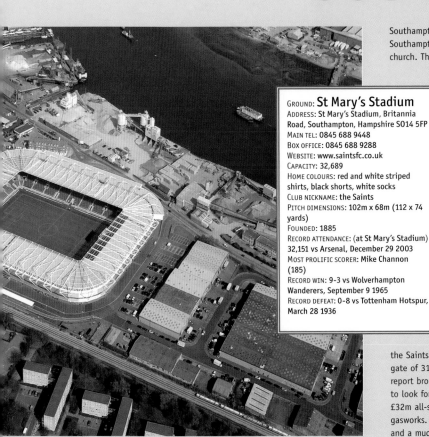

Southampton FC was founded in 1885. They originally called themselves Southampton St Mary's FC, due to their ties with the local St Mary's church. The team played their first games on the site of the County Bowling Club. A year after formation the club moved to the Antelope Cricket Ground, previously home to Hampshire County Cricket Club. The team's success meant that the club became professional in 1894. Two years later they changed their name to Southampton FC, and in 1898 they moved to The Dell. Fortune shone on the Saints, as local fish merchant George Thomas funded the development of The Dell. Both ends were terraced and stands were erected on the east and west sides. The club's fortunes off the pitch were not matched on the pitch and by 1906 there was talk the club may have to leave The Dell as their debts were soaring. The Saints held on and after two years in the Second Division they won promotion to the First in 1922. This success meant they were able to expand the ground, and they began with an £8,000 extension of the East Stand. In 1927 the West Stand was torn down and a new one was erected in 1928. The late 1940s saw high attendances at The Dell and three concrete platforms, known as the chocolate boxes, were fixed above the Milton Road End Terrace. Little changed at The Dell for the following 30 years. During that time the Saints won promotion to the top flight and attracted their record gate of 31,044 in a League game against Manchester United. The Taylor report brought the ground's capacity down to 15,352 so the club began to look for a site for a new stadium elsewhere. In August 2001, the new £32m all-seater St Mary's Stadium was opened on the site of a former gasworks. The totally enclosed stadium has one tier all the way round and a much healthier capacity of 32,689.

GROUND: St Mary's Stadium
ADDRESS: St Mary's Stadium, Britannia Road, Southampton, Hampshire SO14 5FP
MAIN TEL: 0845 688 9448
BOX OFFICE: 0845 688 9288
WEBSITE: www.saintsfc.co.uk
CAPACITY: 32,689
HOME COLOURS: red and white striped shirts, black shorts, white socks
CLUB NICKNAME: the Saints
PITCH DIMENSIONS: 102m x 68m (112 x 74 yards)
FOUNDED: 1885
RECORD ATTENDANCE: (at St Mary's Stadium) 32,151 vs Arsenal, December 29 2003
MOST PROLIFIC SCORER: Mike Channon (185)
RECORD WIN: 9-3 vs Wolverhampton Wanderers, September 9 1965
RECORD DEFEAT: 0-8 vs Tottenham Hotspur, March 28 1936

SUNDERLAND

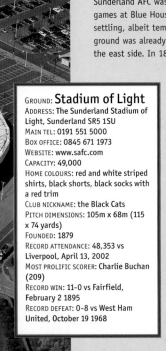

Sunderland AFC was formed in 1879 by Glaswegian teacher Jimmy Allen. They played their first games at Blue House field, close to Allen's school. The club moved four more times before settling, albeit temporarily, at Newcastle Road, the district's best ground at the time. The new ground was already enclosed on three sides, so the club only had to build one further stand on the east side. In 1888 the legendary Tom Watson took over as manager at Newcastle Road. He brought in new players and, after joining the League in 1890, they won three successive championships. The team's success meant increasing support, and it was not long before the club had to look for a new ground. In 1898 the club moved to Roker Park, where the club would stay for 99 years. During the summer two stands were built – the Grandstand and the Clock Stand, the other two ends being left open. In 1908 the capacity of Roker Park was 50,000. The 1920s saw further development; in 1925 the Fulwell End was expanded bringing capacity up to 60,000 and the Main Stand was erected in 1929. March 8 1933 saw a record 75,118 fans cram into Roker Park to see Sunderland take on Derby County in the FA Cup. The Clock Stand was replaced in 1936 and no further development took place until after the war. Roker Park was selected as a venue to stage games during the 1966 World Cup. This led to the pitch being expanded by three yards, while seats were added in the Clock Stand and the Fulwell End was covered. The next major changes came in the 1990s when, following the Taylor report, the club had to decide whether to redevelop or relocate. After a lengthy battle with the nearby Nissan car plant, a new site was found in 1996, on the site of the former Monkwearmouth Colliery. The Stadium of Light opened in 1997, with three two-tier stands on the north, south and east sides linking to the Main Stand on the west. The capacity was expanded to 49,000 in 2001 when the Carling (North) Stand and north-west corner were expanded to three tiers.

GROUND: Stadium of Light
ADDRESS: The Sunderland Stadium of Light, Sunderland SR5 1SU
MAIN TEL: 0191 551 5000
BOX OFFICE: 0845 671 1973
WEBSITE: www.safc.com
CAPACITY: 49,000
HOME COLOURS: red and white striped shirts, black shorts, black socks with a red trim
CLUB NICKNAME: the Black Cats
PITCH DIMENSIONS: 105m x 68m (115 x 74 yards)
FOUNDED: 1879
RECORD ATTENDANCE: 48,353 vs Liverpool, April 13, 2002
MOST PROLIFIC SCORER: Charlie Buchan (209)
RECORD WIN: 11-0 vs Fairfield, February 2 1895
RECORD DEFEAT: 0-8 vs West Ham United, October 19 1968

TOTTENHAM HOTSPUR

Tottenham Hotspur was formed by a group of cricketers in 1882. The team, then called Hotspur FC, first played games on Tottenham Marshes. By 1885 the club had added the prefix "Tottenham" and three years later the team moved to their first proper ground, Northumberland Park. In 1899 the club moved again to a ground owned by a local brewery then called the High Road Ground. Spurs became the first non-League team since 1888 to win the FA Cup in 1901. The club's first major stand, the West Stand, opened in 1909. The stand came complete with a mock-Tudor gable and a year later a copper cockerel perched on a ball was placed on the roof. In 1919 the ground adopted the name of the local station – White Hart Lane. Spurs won the FA Cup for the second time in 1921, and this funded the covering of the Paxton Road End and the Park Lane End. It was not until 1934 that the final terrace – the East Terrace – was built. The East Stand was a two-tier stand erected on top of the terracing, so it resembled three tiers. This stand had a capacity of 24,000 and when Spurs took Sunderland on in the FA Cup in 1938 a record 75,038 fans looked on. The cockerel moved to the East Stand in 1958 in time to see the club go through their most successful era, winning the double in 1961, the FA Cup in 1962 and '67, the League Cup in 1971 and 1973, the European Cup Winners' Cup in 1963 and the UEFA Cup in 1972. In the 1980s the club became nearly bankrupt as the building of the West Stand cost almost double the original estimate. The redevelopment of the East Stand in 1987 again caused crippling debt as costs spiralled. However, the club managed its debts and after adding seats to the East Terrace, the Park Lane Terrace and the Shelf, the new South Stand was built in 1995, and a new upper tier was added to the Paxton Road End, bringing the capacity up to 36,214.

GROUND: **White Hart Lane**
ADDRESS: Bill Nicholson Way, 748 High Road, Tottenham London N17 0AP
MAIN TEL: 0844 499 5000
BOX OFFICE: 0844 499 5000
WEBSITE: www.tottenhamhotspur.com
CAPACITY: 36,214
HOME COLOURS: white shirts, navy blue shorts, navy blue socks
CLUB NICKNAME: Spurs
PITCH DIMENSIONS: 100m x 67m (109 x 73 yards)
FOUNDED: 1882
RECORD ATTENDANCE: 75,038 vs Sunderland, March 5 1938
MOST PROLIFIC SCORER: Jimmy Greaves (220)
RECORD WIN: 13-2 vs Crewe Alexandra, February 3 1960
RECORD DEFEAT: 0-7 vs Liverpool, September 2 1978

WEMBLEY

Sport was played on the site occupied by Wembley stadium as far back as the 1880s when Wembley Park Leisure Grounds had football and cricket pitches and a running track. In 1889 the site's owners decided to build a main attraction at the site and began work on a huge four-legged tower to rival the newly constructed Eiffel Tower in Paris. Work began but was never completed and in 1907 what had been built was dynamited. The first Wembley Stadium was a project devised by the government in 1918 following WWI. Plans were drawn up for a British Empire Exhibition, with a national sporting stadium as the centrepiece. The stadium was originally named the Empire Stadium, designed by architects Sir John Simpson and Maxwell Ayerton; it took just 300 days to complete. George V officially opened the Empire Exhibition in 1924, although the first event held at the stadium was the 1923 Cup Final between West Ham United and Bolton Wanderers. During that game the stadium's official capacity of 126,047 was exceeded and an estimated 200,000 people crammed in to see the game – often called "the white horse final" – because of the famous newsreel footage of a policeman on a white horse vainly trying to control the crowd. The ground was oval-shaped and the pitch was surrounded by a running track. The north and south ends of the stadium had seated stands, while the remaining sides had open terracing. Floodlights were added to the stadium in 1955, and the encircling roof and electronic scoreboards were added in 1963. In 1990, following the Taylor report, the ground became all-seater and had a capacity of 80,000. Apart from this, very little changed in the stadium's structure from its original 1920s design. The stadium has been used for a wide variety of events ranging from England's 1966 World Cup triumph against West Germany to the place where Pope John Paul II celebrated a Mass in 1982. However, its poor facilities, coupled with its inaccessible location, led to calls for Wembley to be closed and a new national stadium built in a more central location. Despite various suggestions for alternative locations, in the end the Football Association decided Wembley was the best place for corporate clients and in 2002 the decision was taken to build a new Wembley Stadium on the grounds of the old one. The first Wembley Stadium was finally closed in 2000 and the iconic twin towers came down in December

2002. The new Wembley Stadium was completed on March 9 2007 when the keys to the stadium were handed over to the Foootball Association. The first ever FA Cup final at the new Wembley was between Manchester United and Chelsea on May 19 2007. The 90,000-seater stadium stages football, rugby and music events, and will also host major athletics meetings. To turn the stadium into an athletics venue there is a removable steel and concrete platform, 6m above the football pitch, with a 400m running track. The most unusual feature of the new stadium, however, is its arch – a 133m (436ft) tall structure located above the North Stand. Made of steel, the arch is 315m (1034ft) long and is the longest single roof structure in the world. The arch supports all of the weight of the north roof as well as some of the south. It sits at an angle of 68° from the horizontal

and can be opened to let light on to the pitch. It is estimated that the London Eye could sit comfortably between the pitch and the top of the arch. The new stadium boasts many state of the art facilities, including two giant screens, escalators, more than 2,000 toilets and, most importantly, more leg room in every seat than there was in the royal box at the old Wembley. In 2012 the new stadium will host the football competition as part of the London Olympics.

WEST BROMWICH ALBION

West Bromwich Albion FC was created by a group of workers from Salter's Spring Works in 1878. More than 100 years after they formed, they are one of only a few English football clubs to have won all three major honours – the League title, the FA Cup and the League Cup. They originally called themselves the West Bromwich Strollers after walking to nearby Wednesbury to buy themselves a ball. The name stuck until 1880, when they changed their name to the more familiar Albion. The club played at five different grounds before settling at The Hawthorns in 1900, so called as the ground was once surrounded by hawthorn bushes. Situated between Birmingham and Sandwell, the initial capacity was 35,500, but when the club bought the ground's freehold in 1913 it began developing the stands. Concrete terracing was installed in 1920 and by 1924 the capacity reached 65,000. Terracing was completed on all four sides of the ground in 1931, the year the club won the FA Cup for the third time and gained promotion to the First Division. In 1937 the ground saw a record attendance as 64,815 watched the Baggies take on Arsenal in the sixth round of the FA Cup. The more familiar stands were built between the 1940s and the 1960s. The East Stand, known as the Rainbow Stand because of its multi-coloured seats, was built on the site of the former Handsworth Stand. Improvements continued to the Birmingham Road End, which was covered in 1964, and the Halfords Lane side. The 1960s also saw the emergence of the Baggies' two most prolific scorers, Jeff Astle and Tony Brown. Following the Taylor report, a £4.15m all-seater stadium was opened in 1995. The Rainbow Stand was finally demolished in 2001 to make way for the new East Stand. When it opened in 2002 to a 1-0 defeat by Grimsby, The Hawthorns became fully enclosed.

GROUND: **The Hawthorns**
ADDRESS: The Hawthorns, West Bromwich, West Midlands B71 4LF
MAIN TEL: 0871 271 1100
BOX OFFICE: 0871 271 9780
WEBSITE: www.wba.co.uk
CAPACITY: 28,003
HOME COLOURS: navy blue and white striped shirts, white shorts, blue and white socks
CLUB NICKNAME: the Baggies
PITCH DIMENSIONS: 105m x 68m (115 x 74 yards)
FOUNDED: 1878
RECORD ATTENDANCE: 64,815 vs Arsenal, March 6 1937
MOST PROLIFIC SCORER: Tony Brown (218)
RECORD WIN: 12-0 vs Darwen, April 4 1892
RECORD DEFEAT: 3-10 vs Stoke City, February 4 1937

WEST HA

West Ham United began as Thames Ironworks, a team set up by Arnold Hills in 1895. Hills was a shipyard owner, and the club's nickname "the Hammers", refers to the tools of shipyard workers. The team originally played at Hermit Road in Canning Town before eventually moving to Upton Park in 1904, four years after renaming themselves West Ham United. The club's ground is actually called the Boleyn Ground, named after a 16th century house that stood next door to the

GROUND: **Upton Park**
ADDRESS: Boleyn Ground, Green Street, London E13 9AZ
MAIN TEL: 020 8548 2748
BOX OFFICE: 0870 112 2700
WEBSITE: www.whufc.com
CAPACITY: 35,146
HOME COLOURS: claret shirts with blue sleeves, white shorts, light blue socks with claret hoops
CLUB NICKNAME: the Hammers
PITCH DIMENSIONS: 101m x 64m (110 x 70 yards)
FOUNDED: 1895
RECORD ATTENDANCE: 42,322 vs Tottenham Hotspur, October 17 1970
MOST PROLIFIC SCORER: Vic Watson (306)
RECORD WIN: 8-0 vs Sunderland, October 19 1968
RECORD DEFEAT: 2-8 vs Blackburn Rovers, December 26 1963

WIGAN ATHLETIC

Springfield Park, Wigan's original home ground, was first used for football in 1897 by Wigan County. Before then the ground was a sports ground with a horse trotting track, a concrete cycle track and a running track. Following Wigan County's demise, a succession of Wigan clubs formed and disbanded, with Wigan Borough being the most successful, lasting from 1919 to 1932. During Borough's ownership of the ground the original stands were replaced and a new main stand created. The Shevington End Stand and the Popular Side Stand were also constructed during this period. When Wigan Athletic formed in 1932, they bought Springfield Park and this remained the Latics' home for the next 67 years. The Latics' first game at Springfield Park was against Port Vale Reserves, which ended in a 2-0 defeat for the home side. The club fought for League status until 1978. During this time the club drew the largest crowd in its history. More than 27,500 fans turned up to see the Latics beat Hereford United 4-1 in the third round of the FA Cup; in the next round the club faced Newcastle United. The Latics finally made it to the Football League after 34 attempts in 1978. They marked the occasion by losing 3-0 to Grimsby Town. The Latics

had mixed success after joining the League. An impressive start saw them promoted to the Third Division at the end of the 1981/2 season. They stared bankruptcy and relegation to the Conference in the face after a bad run of results in the 1992/3 season, but their fortunes were reversed when local businessman Dave Whelan bought the club in 1995. He subsidised the building of a new stadium, then the JJB Stadium, which they moved to in 1999. The new stadium is shared with local rugby league team Wigan Warriors.

GROUND: **DW Stadium**
ADDRESS: Robin Park Complex, Newtown, Wigan WN5 0UZ
MAIN TEL: 01942 774 000
BOX OFFICE: 0871 663 3552
WEBSITE: www.wiganlatics.com
CAPACITY: 25,023
HOME COLOURS: blue/white striped shirts, blue shorts, white socks
CLUB NICKNAME: the Latics
PITCH DIMENSIONS: 110m x 60m (120 x 66 yards)
FOUNDED: 1932
RECORD ATTENDANCE: 27,526 vs Hereford United, December 12 1953
MOST PROLIFIC SCORER: Peter Houghton (62 goals)
RECORD WIN: 7-1 vs Scarborough, March 1997
RECORD DEFEAT: 1-6 vs Bristol Rovers, March 1990

M UNITED

ground. Attendances climbed and in 1913 the new West Stand was built, which was extended in 1925 to a two-tier structure. At this time the South Stand was covered, as was the East Stand. During the WWII the South Stand was severely damaged when a V1 bomb landed on the ground. The 1960s brought sweeping changes to Upton Park, beginning with the covering of the North Bank. Another bay was added to the West Stand and the East Stand was completely rebuilt, significantly raising Upton Park's capacity, so much so that a record 42,322 fans saw the Hammers take on Spurs in a First Division derby in 1970. As with many other clubs, the ground had to reduce its capacity following the Taylor report. In 1991, the club bought land behind the West Stand, which they rebuilt and expanded. However, the club was in financial difficulties, and in November 1991 launched a disastrous bond scheme. Boycotts and pitch protests followed and gates dropped below 16,000. To try and lure fans back, the club slashed the price of season tickets and eventually began redeveloping the South Stand (now the Centenary Stand) in 1993. The Bobby Moore Stand opened in 1994; the new millennium brought further redevelopment to the Dr Marten's Stand and East Stands, raising the capacity of the ground to 35,146. Plans for any further development have now been put on temporary hold.

WOLVERHAMPTON WANDERERS

Wolves formed from a schoolboys' team, St Lukes, in 1877, which then merged with a local cricket and football team, The Wanderers, in 1879 to form Wolverhampton Wanderers. After playing home games at Goldthorn Hill and Dudley Road, in 1889 the club moved to Molineux. A grandstand was built which could seat 300 spectators with shelter for a further 4,000 fans. Wolves played their first League game in 1889 against Notts County, which they won 2-0. Despite boasting a capacity of 20,000, it was not until 1925 that the major stands were built. The first was erected on the Waterloo Road side of the ground. The Molineux Street Stand was rebuilt in 1932 after a gale blew the old cover down. This distinctive structure had a multi-span roof, with a clock mounted in the centre. The 1930s saw the north and south end terracing covered to shelter the large crowds that flocked to home games. During this period, 61,315 fans turned up to see Wolves take on Liverpool, the largest crowd ever recorded at the ground. During the 1950s Molineux was best known for its newly installed floodlights. Top European clubs flocked to the Midlands ground to enjoy the opportunities of midweek evening games that floodlights made possible. In 1978, new legislation led to the demolition of the Molineux Street Stand and in its place a £2m grandstand was erected. This stand almost led to the club folding as they struggled to cope with the debt but in 1986 they were saved by the local council who bought the ground for £1.12m. In May 1990 Sir Jack Hayward purchased Molineux for an estimated £20m, redeveloping the ground into one of the then most modern in the country.

GROUND: **Molineux**
ADDRESS: **Molineux Stadium, Waterloo Road, Wolverhampton WV1 4QR**
MAIN TEL: **0871 880 8442**
BOX OFFICE: **0871 880 8443**
WEBSITE: **www.wolves.co.uk**
CAPACITY: **28,500**
HOME COLOURS: **gold shirts, black shorts, black socks**
CLUB NICKNAME: **Wolves**
PITCH DIMENSIONS: **106m x 68m (116 x 74 yards)**
FOUNDED: **1877**
RECORD ATTENDANCE: **61,315 vs Liverpool, February 11 1939**
MOST PROLIFIC SCORER: **Steve Bull (247)**
RECORD WIN: **10-1 vs Leicester City, April 15 1938**
RECORD DEFEAT: **1-10 vs Manchester United, 15 October 1892**

First published in 2010 by
Myriad Books Limited
35 Bishopsthorpe Road, London SE26 4PA

Photographs © Flight Images

Text copyright © Cassandra Wells

Cassandra Wells has asserted her right under the Copyright, Designs and Patents Act 1998 to be identified as the author of this work.

ISBN 1 84746 344 4
EAN 978 1 84746 344 9

Designed by Jerry Goldie Graphic Design

Printed in China

www.myriadbooks.com